D0894253

Bread

Edited by Rebecca Stefoff

Text © 1991 by Garrett Educational Corporation

First Published in the United States in 1991
by Garrett Educational Corporation,
130 East 13th, Ada, Oklahoma 74820

First Published in 1987 by A & C Black (Publishers) Limited, London
with the title BREAD
© 1987 A & C Black (Publishers) Ltd.

Manufactured in the United States of America

Library of Congress Cataloging in Publication Data

Baskerville, Judith.
    Bread / Judith Baskerville ; photographs by Ed Barber.
    p. cm.—(Threads)
    Summary: Discusses bread, how to make it, and how to use it for
everyday things and for celebrations.
    ISBN 1-56074-001-9
    1. Bread—Juvenile literature.   2. Wheat—Juvenile literature.
3. Bakers and bakeries—Juvenile literature. [1. Bread.]
I. Barber, Ed. ill. II. Title. III. Series.
TX769.B25   1991
664'.7523—dc20   91-18189
                                                        CIP
                                                         AC

Bread

Judith Baskerville

Photographs by Ed Barber

Contents

GEC GARRETT EDUCATIONAL CORPORATION

What goes into bread?

Taste some flour.

Taste a very small amount of salt.

Drink some water.

How would you describe the tastes?
Water is a good drink, but it doesn't have much
flavor. The flour and the salt do not taste very
good at all.

Try mixing them together. Maybe this will
improve the taste? What do you think?

It's hard to believe that this mixture will make something you probably eat every day — bread.

Bread that is good for you.
Bread in all kinds of shapes, sizes, and colors.
Bread with different textures and tastes.
Bread that is eaten almost all over the world.

Flour

Have a look at some different kinds of bread. Taste some with your eyes closed. Can you taste any differences?

Now take a closer look. What color is the bread? Does it have any "chunks" in it? If it does, try to remove them. What do you think they are?

Remember the mixture of flour, salt, and water that you made? It's the flour that gives bread it color and texture.

The flour comes from cereal plants, like these. It's made by grinding, or crushing, the seeds of the plants.

Oats

Rye

Millet

Barley

Corn

Wheat

Seeds (sometimes called grains).

Have you ever noticed the names of these plants on boxes of breakfast cereal?

4

You could try grinding your own flour from
cereal plants. You will need some cereal grain
(you can buy wheat grain from health food
stores) and a tool for grinding. Try using two
stones or a rolling pin. You'll find that it's very
hard work. That's why, nowadays, most flour is
made by machine. The grains are ground between
huge steel rollers.

Almost all the different kinds of flour you see in the grocery store are made from wheat grains, like these.

Try cutting a grain of wheat down the middle. If you look at it through a magnifying glass, you'll see that it has three main parts.

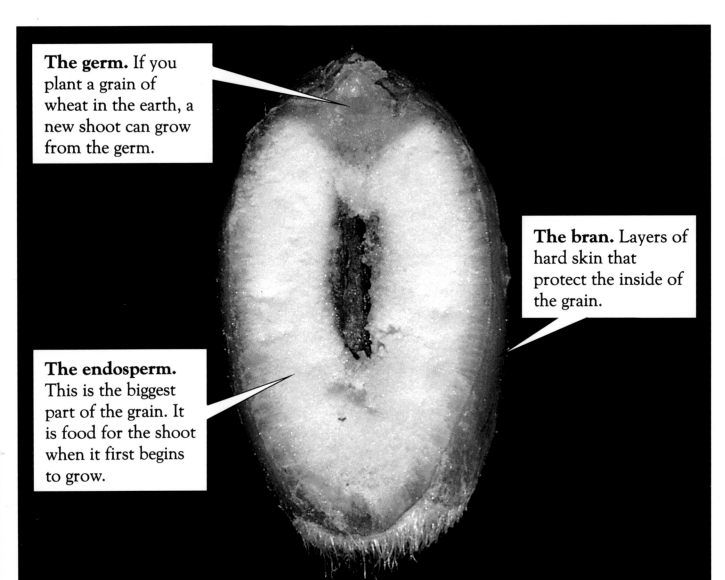

The germ. If you plant a grain of wheat in the earth, a new shoot can grow from the germ.

The bran. Layers of hard skin that protect the inside of the grain.

The endosperm. This is the biggest part of the grain. It is food for the shoot when it first begins to grow.

These flours are all made from different parts
of the wheat grain.

Brown flour is made from
nearly the whole grain, but
some of the hardest bran
skins have been removed.

Whole wheat flour is made
from the whole grain

White flour is made from the
endosperm of the grain.

What kinds of bread could you make from these flours?
Try to imagine the color and texture of the bread.

What makes bread rise?

There is something that makes wheat flour special and different from nearly all other cereal flours.
These flat breads, called rotis, are made from wheat flour and water. Have a close look at them.

Can you see that the cooked roti on the right has puffed up? It has risen slightly. When wheat flour is mixed with the right amount of water, a new substance, called gluten, is created.

Try making gluten

You will need

Oven, set at 450°F
Safety note — Be sure to get permission from an adult before using the oven.

2 tablespoons of water

2 oz. of flour

How to do it

1. Mix the flour and water together to make a smooth dough. Roll the dough into a ball and soak it in a bowl of cold water for half an hour. Then gently fold and squeeze the dough under a running tap.

2. After about five minutes, you will be left with just the gluten. What does it look and feel like?

3. Cook the gluten in the oven for about 20 minutes. Let it cool and then have a good look at it. How much does it weigh? Try cutting it open.

Gluten stretches, rather like chewing gum. When it is heated, it blows up like a bubble. Imagine lots of tiny bubbles being blown up inside the roti. No wonder the roti rises when it is cooked.

9

Look at all the bubbles in this slice of bread.

The gluten in wheat flour makes bread rise a little bit. But something else is often added to bread, to make it rise even more.

Can you tell which of these breads have been cooked with this extra ingredient?

Usually, a special plant, called yeast, is the extra ingredient that makes bread rise, although chemicals are sometimes used instead.

Like all plants, yeast is alive, and it needs food, water, and warmth.

If you want to see how yeast works, try this.

You will need

A little warm water

2 teaspoons of sugar

2 teaspoons of fresh yeast

Mix them all together and watch what happens.

After 10 minutes, bubbles appear round the edge of the bowl — keep watching. After 40 minutes, the surface will be frothy.

The yeast is feeding on the sugar. As it feeds, it makes the bubbles of gas that you see.

When yeast is mixed with flour and water to make bread, it feeds on part of the flour and makes bubbles of gas in the bread. This is what makes the bread rise. Try making your own bread and see what happens.

How to make bread

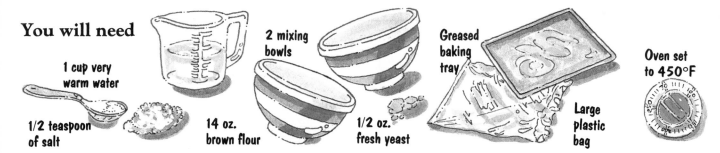

You will need

1 cup very warm water

1/2 teaspoon of salt

14 oz. brown flour

2 mixing bowls

1/2 oz. fresh yeast

Greased baking tray

Large plastic bag

Oven set to 450°F

How to do it

1. Mix the flour and salt together in a bowl. In another bowl, mix the yeast with the water. Keep stirring until all the yeast has mixed in properly.

2. Make a well in the flour and pour the yeast liquid into it. Then mix them up. This makes the dough.

3. Sprinkle some flour on a clean flat surface. Then tip the dough on to it. Fold the dough in half and press down on it. Keep folding and pressing until the dough stops being sticky. This is called kneading, and it will take at least 5 minutes.

4. Cut the dough into 10 pieces and roll each piece into a ball. Put the balls of dough on a greased baking tray and put the tray carefully into the plastic bag. Then leave the dough in a warm place to rise.

After about 50 minutes, the dough will have doubled in size. The yeast has done its work. Take the baking tray out of the plastic bag.

13

5. Bake the dough in the oven for 10-15 minutes. The heat will stop the yeast from working any more. The yeast helps to give baking bread its lovely smell.

Let your rolls cool. Then you can eat them.

Remember tasting the flour, salt, and water?
What a difference!

You can use your bread dough to make lots of different things to eat. Here are some ideas to get you started. (There are some recipes at the back of the book.)

Roll the dough flat and make pizzas.

Try adding dried fruit and nuts.

Put seeds like poppy or sesame on the top.

How the sandwich got its name

You could use your rolls, or different kinds of bread, to make sandwiches. Swap ideas with your friends. You might be able to invent a brilliant new kind of sandwich.

The sandwich got its name from a man called the Earl of Sandwich, who lived about two hundred years ago. He enjoyed playing cards so much that he never wanted to stop for meals. One day, he asked for a piece of meat to be served between two slices of bread, so he could eat while he was playing. The name sandwich has stuck ever since.

In the bakery

In your family, do you bake your own bread or buy it at a supermarket or bakery?

This supermarket has a bakery behind the shop. The bakers start work at three o'clock each morning, so that the bread will be ready when the supermarket opens.

The baker starts by mixing up the yeast, flour and water in a big machine. Then he takes out a lump of dough and cuts it into pieces.

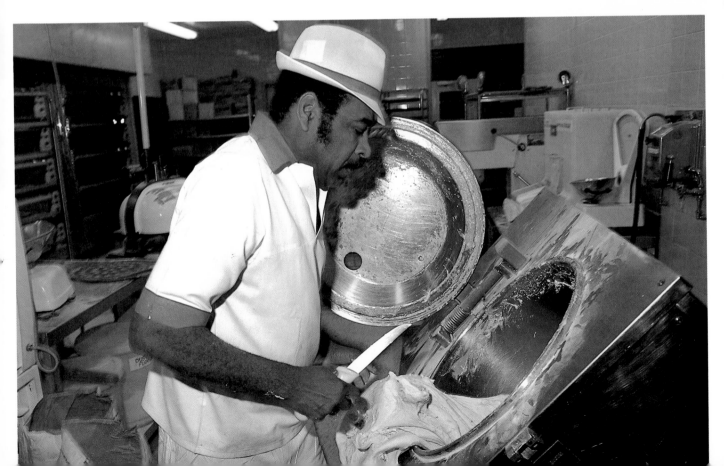

DIVIDER SCALING
WEIGHTS

LARGE BREAD   950 g

SMALL BREAD   470 g

FRENCH STICKS   520 g

BATCH BREAD   300 g

CHECK WEIGH AT LEAST THE
FIRST "5" AND LAST "5"
DOUGH PIECES PER DOUGH AND
1 IN 10 DURING RUN.

Each piece of dough must be just the right weight to make a loaf. Inside this machine, the dough is kept warm, so it rises just a little bit.

Some of the loaves are sprinkled with seeds, or decorated with different patterns.

The loaves are put into a big steam cupboard, and the warm air and steam inside make the bread rise. Here's the bread being taken out of the steam cupboard.

Now the loaves are ready to go into the oven.

19

The baker keeps checking the loaves to see if they are ready.

When the bread is cooked, it is stacked on racks to cool, and then goes straight to the store.

Slicing and wrapping

Some of the bread you buy in the shops is made in big factories, like this one. The bread is cooked in huge ovens and goes down a conveyor belt to be sliced and wrapped. Then it is taken by truck to different grocery stores and supermarkets.

The companies who make and sell this bread put their own design on the wrapping. Look at some different types of wrapping. Can you find any facts written on them? You could design your own wrapping and make up a catchy name for your loaf.

21

Bread with everything

Bread goes well with so many different things.

Bread pudding

Roti with dhal

Pizza

Pita bread with kebabs

A hamburger with a bun

Toast and marmalade

How many times have you
eaten bread this week?

Bread for celebrations

Bread is so important to us that it is often made for special occasions. Here are two different kinds of bread made for festivals.

Matzos, which Jewish people eat at their Passover celebrations.

A harvest loaf, which some Christians bake for Harvest Festival.

Have you been to celebrations where bread has been served? Was it an important part of the celebration?

We eat bread so often that it seems ordinary, but your next bite should give you a lot to think about.

More things to do

1. Try making a fruit and nut loaf. To make the dough, use step 1-3 of the recipe on pages 12-13. Put the dough in a greased plastic bag and leave to rise for about 1 hour. Then add 5 oz. of chopped dates, raisins or chopped dried apricots; 2 oz. of chopped walnuts; 1 oz. of confectioner's sugar; 1 oz. of butter or margarine. Squeeze and work these into the dough.

Make the dough into a loaf shape and put into a large, greased loaf tin, cover and leave to rise again for about 45 minutes. Bake in a hot oven, 425°F, for about 50 minutes. Cool on a wire rack. Remember always to get permission before using the oven.

2. Think of some experiments to try when you are making bread. Think about the weight and volume of the bread. Talk about your ideas with your friends before you start.

3. Bread that is cooked with an extra ingredient to make it rise is called leavened bread, and it is usually cooked in an oven. Flat bread is called unleavened bread, and it is usually cooked on a hot surface, like a griddle or heavy frying pan. Next time you go to the supermarket, see how many different kinds of leavened and unleavened bread you can find. Don't be afraid to ask the names of the ones you don't know.

4. Try cooking some flat bread. Rotis are quite easy to make. Ask an adult to help you because you will need a hot stove.
You will need: 3-1/2 oz. of whole-wheat flour and 3-1/2 oz. of plain white flour; 2/5 cup of water; a bowl; a heavy non-stick frying pan; a rolling pin.
How to do it: Mix the flour and water together and knead for about 5-10 minutes. Cover the bowl of dough with a damp cloth and leave for 20 minutes. Then roll the dough into 12 balls. Flatten each ball and roll out on a floury surface to make a flat circle about 5 inches across. Heat up the frying pan and then put in a roti. Cook for one minute each side. To make the roti puff up, you can put it under a hot grill for a few seconds, or press the edges gently with a tea towel.

5. Bread helps you to keep fit and healthy because it contains vitamins, minerals, and fiber. Look at the labels on wrapped bread and try to find out more about what it contains.

Index